Lake Mattawa 2020

LAKE MATTAWA
2020

a pandemic, a small cemetery, and a month alone

Kathy Kramer-Howe

Haley's
Athol, Massachusetts

Haley's
488 South Main Street
Athol, MA 01331
haley.antique@verizon.net
978.249.9400

Photos from the collection of Kathy Kramer-Howe.
Cover watercolor by Kathy Kramer-Howe.
Copy edited by Mary-Ann DeVita Palmieri.
Special thanks to Janice Lanou.

International Standard Book Number, paperback:
978-1-948380-50-8

International Standard Book Number, ebook:
978-1-948380-51-5

Library of Congress Control Number: 2021949183

for Denise D. Daup • 1953-2021
my friend and colleague in bereavement counseling,
who more convincingly than anyone else
encouraged me to share my poetic voice.

Denise savored poetry for its capacity to
open the heart and provide words to
things of ultimate meaning and
for its healing potential.

Thank you, Denise.

Contents

Photos

Life's Links

a foreword by Sally Howe

As the poetry of Kathy Kramer-Howe reveals in *Lake Mattawa 2020,* we three sisters—Lynn, Kathy, and I—spent most of our growing-up summers at our cottage, locally referred to as a camp, on Lake Mattawa in Orange, Massachusetts. There we learned to swim, row a boat, play croquet, and get along with others. The small cottage provided a gathering place.

Our summers together there are embedded in our hearts and settle us now when we are there. Thus, when Kathy stayed by herself in the cottage during 2020 and the COVID-19 pandemic, she was not really alone.

At the camp during our childhood summers, we would often be ten people with one bathroom and a porcelain portable potty for upstairs. We sisters washed the dishes: Lynn might wash, Kathy dry, I put away in the cupboard. Before the seventies, all we used was lake water for showers, so we learned to be hardy.

Lynn, the oldest, took charge when the parents were involved in croquet. She made sure I didn't wander into the lake and cuddled me after a chill when I was cold. We learned to spend our evenings reading and being together. So when Kathy spent the month at camp there was a lot to draw upon.

Kathy has always been a writer. I even coaxed her to finish my college entrance essay. She dons a cloak of many colors, including that of an artist of stained glass and watercolor. In *Lake Mattawa 2020,* she applies her golden touch to poetry. Kathy finds the junction of inner and outer spaces. Her poems flow easily through memory, the current moment, and the eternal. Life's links join together and wrap around the jewel of camp, Lake Mattawa, and our common past. Her poetry lifts from specific memories embedded in place and rises like the mist to reveal universal belonging.

Four generations have left their imprint on the camp. Our dear Gramps had suppers of Grapenuts at the kitchen table, and we shared family reunions and saw the venerable maple tree with its rope swing become a stump displaying a cascade of petunias. All find presence in *Lake Mattawa 2020.* Kathy's poetry gathers underlying energy and shapes it into form at once evolving and unchanged. I encourage all who read Kathy's collection to bathe in its waters.

I often interrupted Kathy's month of solitude at the camp by banging the screen door and entering with barking dogs. There from the window-lined porch, she sat at the table looking at the lake and North Ridge beyond, the arc of the hill reflected in the water. Every day, she disciplined herself to produce a poem inspired by a passing heron or childhood memory. Thus, poem by poem, her creative spirit sought to find grounding to her feelings.

Lake Mattawa 2020 is a travel book of poems journeying through sunshine and storms, day and night, from stationary to wandering, from lost to found.

As you read, sit next to Kathy at that table and delve into her poetry.

The sweet cottage was a place of happiness for my father, John, and later for my mom, Lee, and us daughters, my sisters Sally and Lynn and me (just Lynn and me here: Sally wasn't born yet).

August by Myself in the Family Cottage

an introduction by Kathy Kramer-Howe

In the first summer of COVID-19, I spent August by myself in our family cottage on Lake Mattawa in the town of Orange, Massachusetts. The red-painted shingled cabin, which we always referred to as the camp, has been in the family since about 1920. My grandfather Frank A. Howe purchased it as a summer getaway when my father was a boy. Gramps was a prominent citizen of the small town on Millers River, president of Orange National Bank. His tastes were simple, and he loved to make the short drive after work from the bank to the camp and breaststroke in the lake wearing his porkpie hat. The sweet cottage was a place of happiness for my father, John, and later for my mom, Lee B. Howe, and us three daughters, my sisters Sally and Lynn and me.

A pleasant body of water nestled in round, forested hills, Lake Mattawa is small enough that a child can safely set out in a canoe but large enough for an adult to feel accomplished when swimming across. As part of Quabbin Reservoir watershed, Mattawa has had limits on its development starting in 1988. Gone are the waterskiing, speed boats, and smelly oil slicks of my youth. Instead, kayaks and silent fishing craft float by, and the lake hosts a nesting pair of eagles, a loon or two, and a ghostly great blue heron.

My husband, Rick, was supposed to come with me, but the pandemic got in the way. Our house sitter in Phoenix suddenly backed out of the arrangement, and Rick stayed home to watch our two cats and property.

In unexpected solitude, I resolved to write a poem each day. I swam, walked up Lake Mattawa Road or over to the Orange Holtshire Cemetery, and occasionally had meals with “safe” friends or family. Every morning on the screened sleeping porch, I put my experiences at the lake into words. *Lake Mattawa • a pandemic, a small cemetery, and a month alone* is the result.

Everything greets me with kindness.

Return to the Cottage

This time, I arrive alone to an empty cabin.
The old key clicks in the blistered door.
Everything greets me with kindness:
maple wood ashes in the hearth,
lake water smelling like new corn,
books crowded tight, Morris chair,
red leather-bound complete
Shakespeare, inscribed in 1901
by my nineteen-year-old grandmother.

On the mantle: brass Ganesh,
grey images of uncles in uniform,
dangling rusted bugle, broken
pottery Hindu Shiva, toy
soldier, studio portrait of my young
mother posed in toe shoes,
pink tulle, pained smile.

My family was most happy here
during the postwar summers
when we were fierce at croquet.
We picked pink worms
from shovelsful of black earth
by the brook, yanked small fry
from underneath the dock.

His hands under tummies, my father
taught us to kick, dead man's float,
dog paddle, dive, control a canoe,
and not fear the natural world.

Each summer I find hanging
on a hook my mother's faded
red chamois LL Bean shirt.
I put it on like skin.

A great grey tent of rain charges across the lake.

Too Soon

A great grey tent of rain
charges across the lake.
It batters the awning,
gouges tiger stripes
into the water surface.
Eight Canada geese plow
nonchalantly into the mouth
of the storm.

I traveled thousands of miles
during a lethal pandemic
to be here, but it's too soon,
I think, for a hurricane.
Even a goldfish needs time
to breathe new water.

Parts of me have not yet
found each other,
like geese in missing-man formation
calling now, hidden behind the rain.

Bringer of Storms

The end of a shallow night,
pillow solid with sweat,
lake agitated, chained buoy bell
clanging against the oak.

On pewter-hued water,
Canada geese parade
into the brisk chop. Dark
stains advance at them.
Brace your sails for a gust,
my father used to say.

The Greeks gave each wind
a personal lord: Boreas
from the cold north, Eurus
of the autumn east, Zephyrus—
spring's west breeze, and
Notus, who rides today,
south wind of late summer,
bringer of storms.

Behind him rumbles the flank
of tropical storm Isaias
on its drive to the sea. Limbs
will topple. Tonight,
geese will shelter.
No one will cherish me.

After Fleeing the Storm

I fled the cottage last night,
my resolve worn down by the wind–
the long arm of tropical storm Isaias
strafing lake chop from the southeast
straight into my teeth, drowning
branches, tossing chairs off docks.

I threw laptop, nightclothes,
and flashlight into a shopping bag
and crept to my sister's safer place,
weaving the rental car through tree litter
wet and monstrous in my beams.

Now in the quiet predawn,
I take a mug of tea and cushion
onto her wet deck. The lawn
is hung with mist.
Five ravens cross overhead,
bawling as they strive
against the sky. I hear
the fan-crack of wings.

In the silence,
a tarnished silver moon
bows low in the west. The sun
drives his winged, golden horses
toward earth's dark, rolling rim.

The moment seems ruled
by a god who catches it
in one open hand and with the other
releases it like a wish.

Rescue

A copy of *Pinocchio* lay on the cherry secretary
where items rarely move until they are ready.
This 1946 edition was read to me at bedtime,
odd illustrations of a wooden/human boy,
English cadenced like another language.

Pinocchio tried to be good and always failed,
his world growing more and more dangerous.
He broke every promise, was beaten, stripped,
robbed, hanged, enchanted into a donkey,
and almost drowned before a fairy rescued him.

Now I need a rescue from this pandemic.
Masks, gloves, hand-wash, distance,
suspicion, and anger fill the world. Risk
is everywhere and riding a plane a sort
of death wish—people say their goodbyes.

Yes, a rescue is required. May serenity
of lake, hills, sky touch me, soften
this armor, show me a safer world.
May the buoyancy of kindness
turn me back into a real girl.

All This Otherness

From the porch wall of windows,
endless lake backed by a green
swell of woods where a glacier
slowed eons ago, shed its load.

Sky pearl, water nacreous,
streaked with olive and alabaster
like an artist's palette board.

There is too much poetry here.
Two silvery boats on one line
glide like twin compass needles
pointing into the wind.

Is it my own shadow
that wants to be awake at three?
I need to listen closer, discover
how to be with all this otherness
that is not other but instead
a conversation I have forgotten.

Watch a Lake

To watch a lake
is to catch air at play.

Today leaves hang limp.
Only verges of water
lie flat and still. Between
them, a broad current hurries
southeast to northwest.

Now a contrail with no bird
or boat in the lead
cuts across the flume
toward no destination.

The Visit

After feeding in the shallows
this morning, a gander,
broad and sturdy as a barge,
stops, turns suddenly in front
of the dock, stares up at me.

Soon four geese sidle close,
scull in place.
Alien and riveting as periscopes,
they peer at the porch window.
I watch them watching.

In the quiet, something
works on me and the geese.
Now I can ask, even if
I don't entirely mean it,
for freedom.

Because Tryphena means delicate

Because Lydia outlived her Elihu by only two years,
in their late seventies,
in 1854.

Ode to a Small New England Cemetery

After Thomas Lux

There is a land of pure delight
where friends once parted shall unite
and meeting on that blissful shore
with fond embrace to part no more.

—"Gravestone Poem"
Anonymous

That they lived, ran the course, in this town is reason
to walk among them, speak their names—
cushion your footfalls
on spongy moss above them–that,
for them,
means remembrance. Because Rebecca lasted
ninety-four years, five months. Because Tryphena
means delicate and on June 30, 1859,
at the age of eighty-eight, she broke apart.
Because Lydia outlived her Elihu by only two years
in their late seventies,
till 1854. Because Ruhamah was the relict
of Josephat for twenty-two years.
Because when they heard their names,
they turned and smiled.
Because they married, for love or not,
and shared a narrow bed.
Because she felt life in her belly
and brought it into the world.
Because in their stiff, black clothes
they sang hymns on narrow pews.
Because when they hear their names,
they turn and smile.

Alone in Fred's Cottage

Only as I walk away
do I notice reluctance
to leave the book of poems,
rocking chair on painted planks,
broad screens facing the lake.

Artfully simple rooms
have kept alive a whispered
conversation between pines
and timbers, breezes
and breathing. Presence
had settled comfortably
at the table, on bunk beds,
in window-screen openings.

It was enough to sit,
speak a few poems, feel
the contentment of trees,
for me to join
an ancient communion.

I was invited to allow
being to expand into air,
time into experience.

Marconi Beach, Cape Cod

Masks up, we edge by each other
down a sandy stair to the beach.
Like bands of hunter-gatherers,
we are slung with folded chairs,
hung with totes. We tug a wagon
stacked with bright towels
and carrying a rheumy old dog who,
if left behind, would bray
like a bull seal.

Under our umbrella's pentagon
of shade, we crowd three women,
a cooler, bags of books,
and two more dogs.

We must fortify
our place with stone cairns,
a twelve-foot circle, before face masks
can come off. We glare at new refugees
who trudge across our border.

When we walk the tidal line,
waves hurry after like rattling crabs,
never catching up. The sea
speaks ceaselessly and blood pulses
in the inner ear. A black, glistening
seal head surfaces just offshore.

Heavy with beach narcotic,
people drop on the warm sand.
Masks slip off. Territories are unguarded.
We have come to forget
what we have done to the world,
what we can still do
to each other.

A Glimpse

She entered my room
in the grey of dawn
to retrieve her dog
from the bed. A waxing
moon gleamed wet
through dormer windows.

She would say
she was not yet hatched,
warm from her covers.
Her face was wholly
innocent of her life,
the long entanglements
of sisterhood. Eyes
solemn and trusting,
lips soft, unsmiling.
Skin unlined, lambent.

I could have gathered her
like a dazed child,
held her as I never
did when we were young,
could have wept
with tenderness
breaching my heart.

Porch Spider

I have befriended a spider,
though she doesn't know it.
Master weaver, her web
spans two hanging pots
of begonias and the porch
overhang. Her lines are tight,
symmetrical. Scrambling
along the rigging,
she resets them each night.

After dark, she appears,
chubby and painted,
in the epicenter.
I turn on the porch light
to lure tiny bugs
that she races to bite,
spin, and pin like French knots.

Yesterday, I unglued
a large grasshopper
that she had not yet encased.
It sprang onto my head
before leaping away.

Spiders used to be décor
for my hair when I was small,
especially leggy black
and yellow garden spiders.

With so few left, insects
as well as spiders,
I celebrate each perfect
morning web, offer
my apologies.

Forecast

When you wake today,
the sky will be tufted batting
as far as you can see.
Later, water will drop
on roof and skylight,
grass and lake.

Walk your hill. You will spot
tiny empty booze bottles,
jumbo crushed cups,
just the tail, bristled with fright,
of a chipmunk, the back
half of a small fish, gnawed.

On both sides of the road,
tangled vines and ivy
crawl toward the pale light.

Imagining some dominion,
you will forget a hundred times
today that all this happens
with or without you. It does.
With no more right to be here
than the chipmunk and fish,
you nonetheless belong.

You are impossibly alive.
Everything is given for that.

Welcome to the forecast.

Murder of Turkeys

They are out for forage
in a browse below the road.
Brush cutting has opened
space for low, seeded things.

The tom and I meet eyes.
He leads five hens
high stepping up the rise,
their snoods scarlet
in strobing afternoon light.
One or two settle
their feathers slow and heavy
like laundry tumbling in a dryer.

A rafter of turkeys,
Meleagris gallopavo silvestris,
solemnly gain ground.
How easy it would be
to shoot them, turn them
into tattered heaps.

They never should have caught
my eye, a kind of taunt
to someone like me. Remember,
Homo sapiens killed off
all our hominid cousins.

On the isle of Flores, we eliminated
Homofloresiensis, just three feet tall
like these turkeys. Small, peaceful,
brown skinned, they too foraged
in clearings. I picture six of them
watching me over their shoulders,
reaching for the timberline.

Mother's Casita Sofa

Broken springs, excelsior batting
preserve the impress of your hips
on the ancient casita sofa,
its green canvas torn,
rusted metal frame.

A breeze off the lake
stirs traces of your perfume,
Chanel No. 5, maybe Coco.
You were a Chanel girl.

Twelve years ago, you wheeled
your walker here: your final summer.
I covered you up.
The throw still lies over the back.
It features salient landmarks
of Orange, Massachusetts, 1868:
Grout steam car, New Home
Sewing Machine, Wheeler Mansion in 1903
and Memorial Library.

Smalltown beauty with arched brow
married smalltown Dartmouth man,
and together you took on the world,
all the continents, many seas.
Yet it was here on this small lake,
too minor to appear on the throw,
snuggled onto an aging sofa, that
you truly came home, didn't you?

Legacy

Up the rise from the water,
my niece and her two blond daughters
poke marshmallows at the outdoor fire.

Sun-shot smoke obscures them,
revealing instead my sisters and me,
skinny towheads fishing
with our own marshmallows
sixty summers ago.

Sauntering past the fieldstone chimney,
my young father appears. Pipe
clamped, he scans the lake for breezes,
never quite looking down
from a horizon he prefers.

Behind him smoke soars like scenes
of war he never talked about. It's as if
he never sat, night after night, under
the navigator's dome on a PBY patrol bomber
low over the Pacific, never broke
open a beer when his crew landed
safely one more time.

He'll rig a sail on the Grumman canoe,
set off reading gusts on the water,
as committed to all he is given
as my niece's two youngsters,
now dancing on the croquet lawn,
leaping wildly to what they hear
as life's silent whoop.

I light the old stone fireplace
as my father and his father loved to do.

All the Joy I Need

All the joy I need
wells up right here—
slow evening on the lake,
syrupy light dragging her hem
across drowsy dark hills.

Waters smooth and hammered
advance, vanish into each other.
On the neighbor's dock,
two boys flail with foam lances.

I light the old stone fireplace
as my father and his father loved to do,
feed the ancient god twigs
and litter, get drunk on its fragrance.

Perfections I've conjured, longed for
and mourned, drift off with the smoke.

Happy Fishing

Where the road meets the lake,
a young man has just parked
a black pickup,
lifts out his two-year-old son.

As he turns to get tackle,
the boy sees me walking.
He brandishes his small rod,
waggles the five-inch
plastic fish hooked on the line.
"Going fishing," I smile.
"What fun! Happy fishing!"

I walk on toward the cottage
and cannot stopper my delight.
Bait the hooks.
Throw out the lines.
What you catch
will be something
that already belongs to you.

Petunia

I exist for this.

In my hand, I cup
the hot pink petunia,
petals sticky, fragile
as a moth,

consider its breathtaking
boldness and delicacy.

When it speaks within my spirit,
its single acclamation is
ALIVE!

In the certainty of extinction,
a winter coming for the flower
and for me, I want more.

It tells me again,
I exist for this.

You are enriched.

The breeze catches our words . . .
photo by Amber Howe-McCarty

Zigzag

Stepping out the screen door
on still-wet grass,
I carry my Bates College mug
to one of two metal chairs
painted the yellow of old stop signs.
The lake is rough, a brisk southeast
breeze slapping the rumps
of two tethered aluminum boats.

A grey squirrel zigzags
closer and closer until
she scrutinizes from two feet away.
Her front paws tap dance forward,
back ones dig in. I can see
her rosy milk teats, coiled ear,
shivery breaths. Tail lashing,
she turns and walks
straight up a pine tree.

After Margaret joins me,
we drink coffee, nibble
apricot-ginger scones.
Our conversation zigs and zags
like a living thing nosing
for nuggets, scrambling
to heights for the view.

The breeze catches our words,
sends them aloft like those
outsized bubbles shaken
iridescent and wobbly from string nets.
Some bubbles splash
on the grass, some lift,
vaporize, vanish.

Early Apples

I am driving to the cottage
with two Friendly Town pizzas
in the trunk. On the radio,
a guy with a mandolin asks
What is déjà vu, exactly?
Bach's "Chaconne in D Minor,"
he says, is the ultimate déjà vu,
sixty-four variations on a short theme
in fifteen minutes, the duration
of my drive home. At the four-way stoplight,
Main Street meets itself, each portion named
for its cardinal direction.
The squat water fountain,
scolding finger of the Women's
Christian Temperance Union,
is now a dry relic beside the square.
Déjà vu. Then across the bridge
beside yawning brick factories
missing teeth, someone has tethered
an American flag to a horizontal bar.
It struggles against the late afternoon
breeze. Briggs Street, Chestnut Hill,
Lake Mattawa Road. Déjà vu.
Back at the cottage, our pizza party
has devolved into one of those childhood
games where you tasted bitter exile.
Because of COVID, we are sorted into pods
of safe people. I've been thrown out
because I have a visiting friend.
Déjà vu. When I remark
that it seems early for apples,
I learn that it's not too early
if they're early apples. Next
variation, please, in D minor.

Come Calling

Black gravestones greet me
as I enter Holtshire Cemetery.
By now we are friends,
the little greensward an invitation
to settle on a granite bench,
give my solitude some company.

Rows of crooked slabs
are family neighborhoods,
every body given a bed in the house,
carried to it ceremoniously,
tucked into origins.
In death, we all belong.

A few miles away lies
South Cemetery where my name
and dates will be carved
when I move back
with my parents and their parents,
my sisters, my sweetheart.
Do come calling.

My father taught me this.

Forgiveness

Afterwards I see the opportunity
missed. My sister demonstrates
how she builds a fire, spreads
newspaper, then scrunches, knots
some more, adds splits of wood, fat pine—
an artful mix of air and fuel.

My father taught me this, she confides.
I bristle, a child again.
He taught me, too!
She turns away.

Mistakes are lonely, chunks of wood
cut from the tree, not even part of fire–
a collective ecstatic transformation.

What I need is a body pressed
to my back, arms around me
guiding me to the circle again,
reminding me that even the best
we give is usually less
than the world needs.

In the Velvet Sumac Grove

A small child, bones
light as a bird, hair sticky
with sleep, runs along

a hot, powdered road
at the top of the driveway.
Halfway to the cove,

where she knows shining
turtles sun on sodden logs,
she enters the sumac grove.

Grassy bedding receives
her flung body,
laps against her like waves.

Here, light flickers
as through lace, shines
on scarlet, velveteen globes.

Dappled, dancing, quivering
light fascinates, enchants
like a living thing

wherever she finds it as she grows.
When day finally dims,
may this be the last thing to go.

Lift

If first light hadn't won
this morning,
that bird's harsh rapping
would have got me out of bed
with the coffee mug enclosing
my fingers like a warm hand.

The lake surface glassy,
a reflected marbled sky—
diaphanous puffs of mist
meander soundlessly.

An untidy arrow of geese
heaves skyward. Lift,
lift, lift. Heavy bodies rise.

Halfway through August,
light and warmth start to dive,
rap on my window,
get me up.

Lift, lift, lift.
The season is changing.

Goodbye's Leading Edge

Two days before leaving the lake,
I start to hold on. A cleansing wind
rubs the water raw, the color
of a stiff sweatshirt. Trees tall
as hot-air balloons rain loose
branches on the cabin roof.
I want it all to last.

This time, try letting go.
Let go of clouds like cyclists
racing above the water. Let go
of the russet maple tree
on the way to New Salem General Store.
Goodbye, sip of coffee, sister
carefully edging white paint on wood,
bright leaves scattered over grass,
hot pink flounce of trailing petunias,
like a saucy Dolly Parton costume
on the old stump. Goodbye.

Everything precious flares, sputters,
seen in the rearview mirror.
I race forward, goodbye both empty
and brimming like clouds
that dissolve, then condense on the wind.

Send in the Cherubs

Today, the lake is a rococo dome
saturated blue, pastel clouds
edged in pink and a few
pudgy cherubs waving up at me
with self-satisfied smiles.

Cherubs, with your mirth,
your playful insouciance,
show me how to pack,
clean and leave this place.

Waft my woebegone looks
heavenward with your little wings,
your chubby arms,
as you somersault over the dust.
Kiss the top of my head
with your talent for delight.

Return to Holtshire Cemetery in Search of a Name

Late August and a chill
on the lake. Five leaves have fallen,
delicate pink and orange skin
veined with a green, neural web.

Where is the elusive name chiseled
into black stone? I passed it
yesterday, said I'd return.
Now I peer at crooked slate lineups.

Now I peer at crooked slate lineups.

Pelatiah Day, deceased
on my mother's birthday in 1816.
Lansford Merriam, heroic name,
dead at thirty-seven. The Goodnow family,
Elmer born in 1765. Lucius. Noah.
Rhoda. Royal Phinney. Was it
Shubael Briggs?

Even if I recognize the name,
who's to say it will be the same?
That it was chiseled into stone
guarantees nothing,
so many already erased.

I want the husband back home
to be the man I remember
when I left him a month ago
to come to the lake cottage.
But if fungal filaments patiently
dissolve alphabets in granite,
I must factor in the persistence
of forgetting.

When we are back together,
I may have forgotten my casual
unkindness. He may have forgotten
to hide, may say, on the drive home,
"Don't let's argue. I'll cry."
I may remember his true name.

two silvery boats

Acknowledgments

My dear friend Martin Broomberg received my daily poems via email all month. It was meaningful to share them with one other person who, although halfway across the globe, looked forward to them in his inbox.

Rick, beloved husband and anchor, loved and encouraged me from afar.

I am thankful to my family for looking over my Lake Mattawa poems.

Thanks to my writers' group in Arizona, Circle of Writers, COW, for advice on craft.

I am deeply grateful to Marcia Gagliardi, editor and publisher, for wanting to bring my work to life. She loves the greater Quabbin region of north central Massachusetts and promotes it in her publishing decisions as well as in the thrice-a-year journal *Uniquely Quabbin*. The Quabbin region is an area rich in history, stories, and talent. I am so delighted to be one of those voices.

And, of course, I am grateful for the beauty and serenity of Lake Mattawa, Orange's peaceful woods, Holtshire Cemetery, and the cozy cottage, dear to me from childhood, an unbroken river in my life.

Kathy Kramer-Howe

About the Author

Kathy Kramer-Howe is the middle of three sisters born to a small-town couple with soaring, adventurous spirit. After World War II, John Howe joined the newly created United Nations. In the 1950s he and his wife, Lee, took his young family to Iran and then Yugoslavia to live. While immeasurably broadening her horizons, her travels also gave Kathy a certain rootlessness. The summer cottage on a small lake in Orange, Massachusetts, provided her most reliable sense of home. In fact, she eventually married the boy next door from her girlhood on Long Island, New York, who also spent summer weeks at the camp and learned to swim in Lake Mattawa.

After years of teaching middle school in New York City, Kathy settled in the Sonoran Desert of southwest Arizona, earned a master's degree in social work, and found her true vocation as a social worker and bereavement counselor in a large Phoenix hospice. A daily practice of silent meditation, Centering Prayer, and an active spiritual life complemented work with grief and the dying.

Kathy writes poetry to uncover little epiphanies hidden in everyday living. It is a way to be in conversation with ordinary activities like taking a walk or awakening in the morning, to pay attention to what life might be asking of her right now.

Her poems have won prizes in the Wheeler Memorial Library Robert Collén Poetry Competition for a number of years. She summers at the lake cottage she shares with her two sisters.

Kathy and and her husband, Rick, live in Phoenix with seventeen saguaro cacti and two adorable kitties.

Lake Mattawa

end of day

photo by Amber Howe-McCarty

www.ingramcontent.com/pod-product-compliance
Lightning Source LLC
LaVergne TN
LVHW052357100826
845147LV00013B/860

* 9 7 8 1 9 4 8 3 8 0 5 0 8 *